# THE TOWN SCOLD

# THE TOWN SCOLD

## (WASTE: Part One)

by

Judith Johnson Sherwin

"Al cor gentil ripara sempre amore. . . ."
("Love comes always to the gentle heart. . .")
Guido Guinizelli

Illustrations
by
Margaret Lampe

The Countryman Press

TAFTSVILLE, VERMONT

Grateful acknowledgement is made to the following periodicals, which have published some of the poems from this book:

| The Little Magazine | "Argument One," "Aspen Leaves," and "The Town Scold at the Ducking Pond." |
| The Nation | "Noon." |
| Poetry Now | "Analysis." |
| Connections | "A Gentle Heart: Two," "Harvest Home," "Runes for a Bad Day," and "Shake." |
| Nimrod | "Relic." |
| The Antioch Review | "Sonnet." |
| The Mississippi Review | "With a Silver Comb." |
| Painted Bride Quarterly | "La Dolce Vita in Brussells." |
| Sojourner | "A Gentle Heart: Three." |
| The Fiddlehead | "Argument Two: Mirrors." |

The lines in "Renegade" by William Butler Yeats are reprinted with permission from "The Second Coming" from COLLECTED POEMS of William Butler Yeats. (Copyright 1924 by Macmillan Publishing Co., Inc., renewed 1952 by Bertha Georgie Yeats)

WASTE is a three-part sequence, written in New York and in Brussels between 1962 and 1974. THE TOWN SCOLD is Part One of WASTE. Part Two is TRANSPARENCIES and Part Three is DEAD'S GOOD COMPANY.

# TABLE OF CONTENTS

"It came upon them like an armed man. . ."
*A Journal of the Plague Year,* Daniel Defoe


## SUMMER, THE HAYFEVER IN THE AIR /
## BLOWS ME NO GOOD THIS PLAGUE YEAR


look how i made the plague
walk laughing with seven ores
up to you, popped in his veins, walk
with red spots, bignose bombs, shake
a mean beat for you, rattle: *the black
death is throwing a big blast right
next door, baby, want to go?*

you said: *don't give me next door
that death jazz with knobs on, take
it near home, flick on
the real you for me, what you love
(with put the black spot on me) a good lay,
what you hate, the bad lays you get
(with point the bones at me with burst
blisters in the groin) i want to know.*

### IT'S THERE!

look here, i can't breathe
this stuff now: first it was pollen, then
cats, fur, feathers, fuzz, dust, even, hey!
death, the air i can't take in, keeps
my nose so big swollen thick blocked up.

this riff, honey, shake with it, you'll find
it's all the same one damn trumpet sound
blowing to hell and gone, wrists
sticks to rap out how
the dark man rolls drunk
up to harbor. i'm growing fat
ungainly, coming back on you
with more of the same, allergic to
can't / breathe / through
my own snot, that's what, but hear me snort
how one door down, Defoe
plays his big solo just about now
with never lying close offshore
in a stiff, spotted calm. soon
i'll be thirty-two: till
that sweet-toothed bone-picking wind picks up
grind me out something sweet.

## ARGUMENT ONE:

the lady shews how she is forsaken for a piece of wood

now, put me near your chess
pieces, the Queen, near Her  /
see how She surpasses me
point for point, body, soul  /  Her very line
being both straight and lean
contains more grace than mine
and royal, She claims total loyalty. Her mind
is sharper than my human
mind because it's confined
in a many-pointed crown, and hard
the center through. Her eyes see equally
all ways at once, nor can Her heart be ruled
by sight slipped through Her guard
to shake Her to joy or tears,
nor Her face shocked to show what Time has tooled
with patient, cutting years
or Chance has brought to bear
with pressure, for Her face looks everywhere,
selfwilled as they must be who mock surprise.
                                She moves as She will
no farther than She will
and just as far, and east and west the same  /
direction has no name
to Her  /  She is the compass and the winds.


how tell Her that though
i move one way and one alone and see
one line at a time to keep to, i have what
She lacks the wit to know She lacks. Time

M. Lampe

will take Her, She must lose,
be locked in a box like me
but must return to Her central
throne each game  /
She moves not up nor down
but sideways  /  though She hold all
directions in Her crown
She has not power to climb
heaven  /  love, She has not power to fall
as far as hell when you put Her down, can't feel
how Her game ends
       while mine goes on
          as long as flesh will tell.

## HARVEST HOME

when they crack the sound
barrier over us
they whip down chestnuts out of the spreading
tree onto us
         mop
the shells half off

     some formal way of talking i had once
     could divide
     the feeling from the pain
     almost comes back
     ten kilos at least
     to shell but not let stick
     through my fingertips their spines
     then mash then can  /
                    a way
     of language i've lost
     now could hold
     the flood out of the vein
     let only the shape of blood through  /  save
     for winter with roast
     boar  /  a frame
     of thought i can't remember
     could get
     the juice of grief out to you and could keep
     the pulp here safe with me


     on the floor of a kitchen sky
     the mops go by
     a dull brooding
     on some stringy wet birth

# SOON BE OVER

### (a multiple choice)

| | |
|---|---|
| where did you go | swimming pool |
| what did you do | kept cool |
| what did you want (check one) | nothing real / not much / can't tell |
| what did you find | a dead fly / in the water a drowned leaf / a fin / a ball / a small boy / chlorine |
| what did you take | a hard look |
| what did you have | a coke / a feel / good luck after it all |

| | |
|---|---|
| what did you lose | three teeth |
| what did they take from you | a drink |
| what did you break | wind / a glass / a toast / an oath / all hope |
| what did you spill | not one drop / an eyeful of memory / grief |
| what did you not like | light |

| | |
|---|---|
| where did you hide | don't know / underwater / maybe that |
| how did it end | got lost |
| how did it start | forgot |

8

NOON

you, flat
yellow light, that
shine down on ridge and
crease, and fill every deep
place, shellac the most high
relief flat as an antique
majolica
            plate

tell us there is nothing
new under the sun
if we want to find it we'll have to run
into that dead  /
                    heat

## A GENTLE HEART: ONE

stone walls are nothing like it.
you cry all night, all day  /
here you are, you're going to stay
your life makes no sense to you
you'll make me a present of it
like signing over a bad debt
i'm grown hard with longing
for what, i can't say  /
my blood crystalized overnight
into a frosted mineral tree
all splinters. you say my life makes no sense to you.
you're right, i should go, leave you house, husband
     and children.

i don't cry, i don't say
your life makes no sense to me
though maybe that's equally just: i'll make
you a present of that, we'll balance
my withholding against your cry-now-pay-later expense
of dying. you talk of dying. i want to tell you
it can't be all that bad, you've got my man and
   no children.
you sit here and cry while i clean carrots, talk
of killing yourself the way
you talk of going to Paris some day, seeing
old friends, washing your hair, your stockings, setting
    your life in order,
setting me straight. now i'm rotten with desire  /
wet banknotes falling apart in a damp vault.
you can't do anything till you do everything.
if the life makes no sense the underwear's got to stink
in the safe deposit under the bed. *one thing at a time,*
   i tell you

but in the ribbed vault of my mouth
smell i'm not fair to you. you're talking of dying

here, you are dying from day to day to make sense of
     your life
while i think? *i've nothing human in me, i'm all dried
     up.* you total me,
tell me : *you've nothing human in you, judy, you're
     all dried up.*
i want to yell : *damn you, this is my house, my husband,
     stop crying into them,*
*die or don't die, cheap luxury, but at least do some of
     the work here,*
*scrape the carrots.* i want to cry
too, but i've seen how your tears soften you,
                        Camille without TB,
how you're eaten by that generous flow.
tears, easy tears, i know how well they lie
in your oldtime music ; i know, even if i cry
my tears will make me want to puke. see
stone walls are nothing like it, dead souls
are nothing like it, a gentle heart
is nothing like it.

        *look, he hates scenes,* i say.
my anger is coin of the realm ; i won't  /
                 give it away.

## RENEGADE

tell me all i want's
hang on to what i've got  /
tell me what i lack
is what makes you just great  /
the hole in the sight that makes
for sight the extreme
eye that lets light through
though it blind you  /  dear
god             i            try
to, but i can't
see "a shape with lion body and the head of a man. . .
moving its slow thighs" near
here  /  can't locate
that lucifer center where
spins chaos a-reel all set
to come again down
by the riverside round the corner under a
tree to make an end
"an ende an ende an ende of all"
reserves in me
r e n e g a d e  /  just see
                         into the wood

who's there? some
one mean who's there
in me won't answer, can't give
that first that last that lust of
all miracles day, ask
it how you may  /  never
has, never could  /
squats in the heartland of what
i hate and measures it and then
swallows it and holds it
in  /  makes it part of me

i was, you must know,
sullen, ungrateful, cold

dull, a pighead child  /
sergeant major dear, nobody
ever could get a clear answer
from me, there was a hole
in me and not to see
how many miles to the glory road, and it
was sullen and it was dull and it was hollow
echoed back *yessir,* it was
chaos was always dead
empty, was always where
i was, never could see
where it wasn't and hadn't been to go

could see part way in, though.
it's what i know  /  i can
hang a world from that


                      who


   would marry me

## ANALYSIS

says she doesn't like
the way you're always moving the pieces about
the way your fingers tap
out combinations while you talk to us  /
all night sacrifice
and gambit gobble your brain.
let this man go, take that man on,
transfer  the whole department to some sub

someone's immobilized on the back rank
someone's paralyzed by his own might
someone's dead in the corner

                                doesn't like
the clean unthinking speed of it  /  hands
slam down
problems of personnel
trade the accounting boys over the counter
down all the lanes and airways
the big kill

         can't know
              how

i'm in love with chess
no image this

        lie down

in bed each night
with chess. chess dreams, mutters, turns out
new moves, shocks, charges, won't lie still,
in a ravenous haste and joy
of lust measures my loins,
owns my breast  /  dies there

                your hands win
                the exchange even in sleep

## A GENTLE HEART: TWO

a lady walked down a roadbed
tears pocked into her cheeks,
shouting *oh my god what*
*can i tell you i haven't told*
*you twenty times*
        lit up, then told me again
                  *i need a lover two afternoons*
                  *a week, and nights while my husband's gone*
she counted the clicks of the doorlatch to our room,
listened to each match strike, and it made sense
                  *i'd be better for him,* she promised
                  *with a few men under my belt*
                  *with her tears salting his meat*
                  *he'd do more for me / count*
                  *out / aloud / the waste*
                  *stretched on a bed with just one man*
                  *and his children to use up my*
                  *whole life line*

not disinterested, but wise

as if i, not she, were the one
who cries all night, all day
flicks tears into the ash / tray
listens to wheels, listens to rain
lies / late while the children scream
grinds tears out in her saucer, hears the dentist
drill through the floor and into her, lies like sun / slant
feeling across her bed to our wall / listens
to tears creak in the springs while i tighten my thighs

and i should be: here's his dear girl
drinking again while i look on /
i shouldn't have let her stay, she's no friend of mine
there's nothing i want to let go.
bruised guzzling damozel with no grocery list,
and a celebration of thirst,

did i say bruised? set her out in the sun, she'll do  /
a vision with glass and relit butt
she'll flower out of chianti bottles,
break:
      *twenty times nothing is nothing, a blank:*
                    through the carpet.
head bent, knocks at the arched roof, taller than
      candles/love,
each hair smoking kents, she enters, can't hold her out,
      white weeds on fire
at the fingertips of each hand shoot
              and she's got at least fifty of them

## GODDESS

asleep while the children howl and the house burns,
then wakes to crackle her tearsparks over us all,
dead gentle on center with every lingering grief of
      the world
and a glorious ragged consuming gift-gilt-edged
agony in whatever garden she settles in,
girl all awash with thorn flowers of seeing

she's eaten up with what i don't have

and should burn house, children, and man to get:
      that generous greed,
that gentleness which gnaws what it loves, that
      melting violence
going to pieces with its will to suffer
              something, anything  /  sanity
that is mad for lack of reason in the world. . .

lady, my enemy, whom i envy
              rottenly
think of me where you have gone
i think of you with bitter longing always

## RUNES FOR A BAD DAY

thunder and steam, a trail of air
the jets shoot over my roof of hair
sweetheart i have to say
you're not very nice today
you don't shine when you think about me
what it should have been like
     diamonds under my pillow
     to cut you with, the pillow
     to shine you with, a new tooth each
     sunrise  /  to bite you with
                           attention
friends, that was the genie in the smoke
buzzing you

thunder and steam, a blush of rust
the drills dive into my floor of dust
sweetheart i have to say
i shall pick out something to cut
tote up for you someone sweet
to gather for dinner, we'll eat
roses the next day
if they set right     /     like
     you a beggar     i an angel
     you demanding     i dispensing
     you devouring     i descending
     (its virtue is to make you keep up
     a garden of hatchets you'd otherwise drop)
                           attention
friends, that was the genie in the rock
buzzing you

thunder and steam, a flurry of grain
wild elephants flatten my ribs of cane
sweetheart you have to see
how kindly you don't touch me
at least the elephants are normal
this time of year
you bring your old socks here
leave your truelove lying around on the floor
all sweaty expect me to cheer her
when the dog chews her  /  like
     i become a giant clam in heat
     you become a pearlstone rubbed at my root
     you all presence     i departed
     you all heavy     i am empty
                    attention
friends, that was the genie in my loin
buzzing you

thunder and steam, a puff of air
the bombs float into my roof of hair
it's sunrise once again over the old
manse: how come no teeth?

## RELIC

HERE I AM GREAT BIG  /  DINOSAUR LADY ON VIEW
you want to know where they dug me up
and who  /  you want to know
                                (and why  /  hup!
how in the regular flow
of your lavas, the salt set
of your glaciers, the lurid grind
of ice ages over your mountains, the frenzy bite
rock erratics nibbled out
of your shoulders, the licks their tongues made
sly, dipped into your clefts, the changes
of temper, of axes, of height, depth, all that foreplay
of seasons and rockthrusts, that afterglow
of erosion  /  *I* was preserved
alive and belching.


syncline
            anticline
in a rat-race measure my decline
into presence  /  tell me
i should take to drink

                          (outside my fish  /  tank
                          window a red flake
                          of geranium round at the head, thinned
                          to a fishtail, mouth caught
                          on a spider's thread, spins:
                          a minnow  /  hooked
                          in rivers of air: not there.
                          flicks its non-existent tailfin at me, winks
                          its dead eye, says that i
should be extinct.

an occasional relic, a spine,
jaw, teeth, even the completely articulated skeleton
might be ok, plenty
of them in every rockpile

M. Lampe

                              but the display
                              of flesh, blood, muscle, rolling eyes
                              straining for sight, acres of open
                              red membrane and strident appetite, you find
distasteful.
              i agree:
nobody asked for me
and if i asked for you  (all this weight to haul
                              from mudhole to mudhole, not
                              rest this gross tail
                              it
was in some era when  on no flat place in peace
we could be prehistoric, m o n s t r o u s
together, eat the sun
up              /              without sin.

## SONNET

again i won't do what you want, what fun, i'll sit
in the corner and pick my nose, kick the table leg, spill
my milk, if you come any closer to me i'll growl
if i happen to shimmy up near you, be sure i'll spit
as i dance away head held sidewards, a-slant; i'm
    a crouch
of defense, i'm annoyance, an angel, i'm what you feel.
all day i'll crumble, mumbling in my hole,
marrow of love, accounts, actions, how much
i match how you measure me. all night, face to the wall
i'll lie at the ready against you a counterpull
to your hunger and sizzling with lust and cold to touch.
under every smooth of my breast into every heat
of my flank works, grinning, Denial; you can't see
how eager you are to take Her when you take me.

## GIFT

                    this
is a pig woman, a thing
made to provoke fertility
and have none she's all breast
and loin no waist no midground take
her in your hand you can run
your thumb along her lines but not
change them she's rough
touching she's ill
mannered she's all
attitude and no answer look she's good
for you she's what you thought
you loved she wants
to be that

                    sharp, only
an angle, there, in her polished
arm which you deny as it denies
you a curl to her brain
embellished which you don't feel under
your thumb a graciousness asked

                              (of me
                              also which i can't give or be
                              or bend to you
                              if i do
                              it won't be me


this image of refusal wants to be
part of you
dear, she won't go away
until you love her too

## ASPEN LEAVES

### 1

we lay on a grid of rock spread out to grill.
mountains of Colorado served us up
to the sun. we'd flown far
to get to that red rock store
of light from where we'd begun

> "sex-itch sex-itch"
> before we were joined my mother hacked
> at us. that day she thought
> herself no less than objective / did not
> know how deep she felt
> the incision our loving made.
> you took it all in your stride.
> when i stood up a bride
> all her blood ran out

that way, glossy, over the Rockies, the high
teeth of the West that bite
the sky. four aspens dripping at head, at foot,
waited at table at ready and dressed to spill
the world for us.

> they had white diamonds on.
> the earthside of each leaf
> shook out how soon we'd be gone
> in green. the first year gone
> my father poured out thanks
> for making me happy, libations

of his tears, my mother smiled
and showed no stitches. we fought
them, they fought us, we fought
each other and all the broken
skin closed with no fuss.
in that rare paradise winnowed of air
whatever we did shone right. the sun
broke in us, open to all delight.
                         we got there.


2


you're here, you're there, you're lost on a flight
        to Stockholm
the Belgian francs are talking to me again
two hundred Belgian francs strut past me to chuckle:
*the languages we use!*
five hundred and fifty blue-kerchiefed heads nod
at the cleaner's, tell me they can't understand my French.
the children can't understand. we've gone
to another country, we're swinging

ten thousand miles away, don't hear what you say,
but i'll see you. three hundred Deutschmarks a little
the blonder and Aryan for fight will quiver to see
you've gone far from me. the market will whittle
our empire down to the gristle.

> here we come:
> father and mother demanding a rosy welcome
> from people too tired to speak  /
> you determined to make a meal of silence
> with people who can't keep still.

the table was bought in New York, the silver and
    crystal made
in Denmark, the meat cooked in Aspen under the sun

> in Brussels we sat down
> ate venison, chose wine,
> and didn't know when we'd done.

my father wrote you as if a letter could kill,
last winter: investments of spite
our families poured in, our blood banked on,
our gentleness came to  /
and all those years of forebearance, crystals of wise
disguise shaped almost like decency fell down,
without blame, cried: *it's gone bad now. they can't*
    *come back.*
*you won't  /  have them in "your" house.*
> how flowering anger
> climbs you like a vine.
> i'm alone here
far from every friend while you take off for Greece.

26

3

the sun
doesn't move the aspen leaves. it seems
to move in them but if the air lay
still just once it would not move. gently
a shift in the air will move
no other thing yet makes these aspen leaves
shudder. they move by a union
of weakness, the thing they are,
with what the air
gives them to be, and the sun
that doesn't move the leaves, doesn't move in the leaves,
makes them what we see.

> when the trunk cracks down the center
> how shall the tree keep whole
> when the hand breaks the hand
> how shall its works not fail
> when the blood swallows the blood
> what word can the mouth spit out
> when we live on hate
> what life shall our loins shape

we shake, we turn
we turn ourselves to the light
we close our eyes, we burn
we change color, we take off, we fly
through the teeth that wait  /  to chew the sky
we say kind words
we get by

M. Lampe

4

good times, good times  /  with you i shiver and shake
the currency is changing
and i can't talk to you
green grows the lucre on the tree
rustles the word up: everywhere i see
the ones who love me
must hate, can't take, each other. they circle here
in luxury of need
assessing the stock  /  issue i am.
the children squabble and clutch
what their elders dropped in the dust.
my dears, no shift in the air can add
one cent to the value of anyone's share  /
                       paid         /        out

nightly i dream of savages to destroy me
dance bonded on my grave
nightly i dream of messengers to rape me
men big-bellied with trade
in this place Baudelaire went mad
struck dumb  /  my blood
jumps in that rhythm, goes its way
without any part in what my mouth will say  /
i know what joy the celebrants share in the feast.

                        i ask what moves here
                        fifteen years gone
                        is never still, what lives
                        here  /  for me to kill, what
                        here or in me will
                        with perfect love keep still
                        for the fire when i put on
*(and this too i would burn if i could*
                        my gloves of incendiary my boots
                        of anarchist  /

after
we were done we ate of ourselves as others did

## WITH A SILVER COMB

i'm too clever to say it  /  i do it with mirrors
my eyes bend around corners, pluck the cold hall
you knew lay in wait for you out from its dark. i can tell all
about What paces upstairs or the faces next door
not quite nice. sundays you lie  /  drowning in papers,
i can feather Its footsteps close  /  at your ear kneel,
comb your hair; then your sleep will count each rustle the wall
makes, deep, as It burrows, drops, feels Its way to my whisper.

sometimes i've grumbled: *how quick the house becomes*
*to catch us up, spy on us, preen itself in our dreams*
*as if we were moons away.* i nag: *bolt the door*
*before or until the Smell comes.*
                              (only, sometimes,
the old, kind way, i tilt up the great glass, pull a star
or two down  /  to press down your eyelids, wink out in your hair.)

SHAKE!

                shake
shake-shake
        what
ache          i'm
dance                    the plague
ague          i'm        the plague
        in you
ache you
        do
                you
oh
acute
        rage
                hate
shake                    the plague the
you're the               plague the
too

                         the PLAGUE the
                         PLAGUE
shake the                PLAGUE          SHAKE

                                         SHAKE

                         the plague      SHAKE
                         THE PLAGUE

## LA DOLCE VITA IN BRUSSELS

paper profits
    i've got
    a desk, a typewriter,
    a dog, two cats, one with a broken leg,
    two children i talk to
    more often when they're home sick
    half a man

    a house
    and words, words
    to fill it

    you've got
    half a woman here
    half another in the office
    a desk, a company car,
    a ticket to the lac de garde
    you don't want for anything

you don't need me

you need

      an accounting

## A GENTLE HEART: THREE

it seems i've got it all
and you've got nothing. just one sensuous squawl
would change us, instead of this stingy peevishness.
*let me be the one to fall apart,* i say,
but see
how i can't do it, i have no tears in me.


as i got older i grew hard to touch,
wondered at how alike
our voices sounded, how much one like
the other  /  we stank.
i heard you croak out how harsh
a calling it is to do
one thing at a time: strike the match, drink up,
stop the damn tears before they rot you,
ask no more of your will than that:
*twenty times nothing*          new under the sun
                    hear each match strike till it makes sense
                    spreadeagled over a sandpile fixed to a nailbed
*to make death where we are*


lady, my sister, mirror, blood drinker,
man eater, user, gentle heart whom i should be
and love


greet death well from me, we'll be friends one day


if you still live
                    the sun drinking us up

## ARGUMENT TWO: MIRRORS

yes, these are love
poems, bad tempered, awk-
ward, they don't look down on you
like the Eagle of the Rock / unmajestic, not stoic,
    they know
What Lips Their Lips Have Kissed, and they'll squawk
if you leave them in Algiers.

angel-poems may let you think
you can bed with spirit, with pure
intelligence: they'll hint
fine meat spread
for you: numbers, science, gods to eat,
gilt / images carved for your plate,
each night two drops of bitters flown    *(it won't hold out*
                          straight
from the cellar to add relish          *(no more than that*
                          *after all those earthworks*
                          *and starquakes?*
                 but
they lie. look in their eyes, gold and deeper than niles
out of memory, green more shallow than sandy
    graves after
seasons set foot on them, see what they show in
    themselves: your
face. what a waste to show
what any mirror shows. and you won't see your world in
them; your world was me
not made to be made smooth
with spirits and reasons. turn around, turn away, look
deep into me, see what i keep
for you, your source

             underground
no nile but a green slough, impatience
and eyes in their scales, and greedy, take all of
    you: they're
alligators they're dragons they're pterodactyls they're

slimy from dreams and hunger, mud slow, how they've
    got cold lean
calculations on, and every wing can cut
with its webs and clutch you
with leathery fingers: i
am your world, each squawk gives you my voice. this
    plainsong calls
you to slavver, and mate with me. my eyes slash,
    narrow, close-set, mean
mirrors wrong-angled to show you my face, not yours
                     (not
                     brazen, but brutal, but heavy, effacing you
                                     only because
                     in the renaissance of will
that's how lizards grow wise.

look, all you need
to know boils in these mirrors.  say i'm
an angel to show you this and i can dance
on a pin and i can flame on a kiss if you
insist and i can split myself / burn
up zodiacs for you
                     (clumsy my leathery tail my ridged
                     backside smacking the whole
                     world to one side when i walk

# THE TOWN SCOLD AT THE DUCKING POND

when the goodwives knelt at the pump to rub clean
their homespun, every word
tolled *praise God* or some formula of mercy.
she caught no good in it, cursed
the journey to promised godliness she'd gone,
the stiff theocracy
she'd come to instead. and found
once again, she'd said
the worst of it out loud.

home in bed
half the night she scolded her goodman's loins dry
till he swore if any stood up in meeting to name
her witch, he'd join the cry
after her, hotfoot, bring her down. each round
full-throated amen he belled
with the brothers in thanks for their virtues turned
        her around
on her bench, drove her away
from God in him
                or in any such proud men.

once she thought
the Voice out of the whirlwind summoned her forth
to denounce, to vaunt: *I'm no scold,*
*I'm Miriam, I'm called  /*
*now, before all, He bids me stand, shout*

*ugly, unwelcome, my cry.*
*I was made to prophesy:*
*our blessings mock God,*
*being without / charity. never mind my accent,*
*how dry,*
       *my lack of parable,*
*how plain. I can't make it*
*quaint or ornate, you'd take it*
       *then for pure fable.*


so held back not
speech but the final claim
of authority
      not so much for finding the same
pride in her outbursts    (when
           she cursed them
           for cursing she did as they)
but because she couldn't see
herself dressed in lion skin
the claws flung down over
her shoulder or dangling wanton between
her breasts, her hair matted, afire in the wilderness
          though she'd found wilderness
          in plenty to burn in
she'd have laughed her message out of order; scorn
at what she would seem made her less than she had
    to say.


fastened to the stool, hands pinioned down
at her sides, feet narrowly
corded together, the plank teetering, the soaked
hair glued to her nose, her mouth,
nervously silly, she couldn't close her eyes
nor hold her breath nor even then keep peace:
                        spat out
gobs of invective the worse for being wet,
cold, ludicrous, obstinate,

M. Lampe

interrupted repeatedly
      by immersion
        and sneezing
without redemption

all that shuddering
sputtered hour the stool would not
sink under her weight
through the pond's muddy bottom, fix her there,
she envied the folk
stripped and red
danced their lust round the whipping post, envied
    the stripes
they took, envied how cheaply
they bought a hearing, envied the witch accused
would burn honestly and have done with it, prayed
       while her lungs wouldn't let her take
       in water
         seemed to burst
       with the pressure
         of anger within her, around her,
that one of these scoffers might so lose
himself as to call
her witch, burn the fury out of her once for all.

wouldn't tell
them or herself or her God how if she'd not been
roped to the stool she'd have flung
herself down on the ground, rolled, howled herself dumb
for want of a gentle sound,
and kind, to her voice, a blind
heart in love approving all,
a sweet tongue.